Praise for LisaAnn LoBasso's
In The Swollen

"A Poetry Minstrel!" *– Las Vegas City Life Weekly*

"*In the Swollen* seems to break through boundaries over what is acceptable in verse." *– The Blackboard*

"While *In the Swollen* reads as one woman's story, it is truly a story of connection and disconnection, wholeness and brokenness, fantasy and reality. It's about inhaling and exhaling. It's about beginnings and endings. The characters that inhabit your space and the characters that inhabit the pages of *In the Swollen* could very well be drinking coffee together as we turn the pages and wonder, are we looking into a mirror or are we a part of the mirror?" *– Julie Jordon Scott, writer, life-coach*

"She has a dynamic approach to poetry. . ."
– Arts Council of Kern

"LisaAnn LoBasso strikes one as a harried mother of two trying to make ends meet. Like most good poets, she does not act like one. The poems of *In the Swollen* reveal an interior aspect of this normalcy which is both primal and sensual. With its powerful juxtapositions and its reoccurring affirmations of bodily and earthly fluids, her poetry is a poetry of dark light." *– David Nigel Lloyd, singer, poet, musician*

Praise for LisaAnn LoBasso's
In The Swollen

"Trés Hot!" *– First Amendment Poetry*

"*In the Swollen* is a disturbing and darkly humorous collection of poetry that takes the reader into places where angels fear to tread. This book packs a wallop!" *– Maestri Gallery*

"LisaAnn LoBasso creates images with her words that claw their way out of the page and into your head. This is a collection to read, feel, and read again." *– Amber Goddard, Liquid Ohio*

"I would challenge you to read this book then read it out loud to find its physical beauty and its patterns of language. Take part in the poems created by this great poet. Don't be shy. Spend your money here."
— gita lloyd, painter

In The Swollen

poetry

LisaAnn LoBasso

nXpress and the author thank the Artist-in-Residence Program of the
Arts Council of Kern and all financial supporters that contributed
in the support of the publication of this book.

In The Swollen, Second Edition
ISBN: 1-4243-0428
ISBN: 978-1-4243-0428-8
(second edition paperback)

ISBN: 1-4107-0005-4 (first edition e-book)
ISBN: 1-4107-0006-2 (first edition paperback)

This book is printed on acid free paper.

Cover Photograph © by LisaAnn LoBasso
Cover design by LisaAnn LoBasso

www.intheswollen.com
www.lobasso.net

In The Swollen, Second Edition produced through contributions from Nexus
Community Collaboration. Inc., a non-profit facility for literary
and arts-related publications.

nXpress-rev. 04/25/06
1stBooks-rev. 01/06/03

to my cherub baby
to my husband
and to my parents
who never understood my art
anyway

Author's Note

When someone asks me to discuss a poem, I go blank. It is as if I am only the presented face, the one presented as the writer while the real writer hides behind the bushes whispering words that I must record. Often I feel unjustified in explaining a poem. I do not feel I myself know my poems any more vividly than another reader of poetry. Perhaps, I know the emotion experienced during the writing process. For example, I was melancholy when I wrote:

> *Everything that's hard is crumbling*
> *under your weight*
> *squished flat under you*
> *like a lonely cockroach in eighths.*

However, when I simply state that I was melancholy; this statement undermines the value of the images in my poetry, and underestimates the power of poetry to be evocative.

I don't follow the idea that my poems are mapped out and specifically work to grab the reader with only one purpose. On the contrary, I believe a poem is layered with themes and ideas so rich, like a painting, that it is impossible to expositorily explain a poem completely. Creativity is often unpredictable and unexplainable, yet a poet is continually asked what was intended, what was meant by an image, what is happening in the poem. Often my response is "I don't know." Many people may feel this is an escape from discussing the issues in the poem, yet, often it is the simple truth. I cannot guarantee any formula that helps the reader examine a poem and understand it, because ultimately I believe a poem is never totally understood, even by the poet himself, but perhaps, if the poet is lucky, it is felt in the gut.

I will not try to explain specific images or complete poems. I am, as a poet, aware of changes in my writing over the last few years. I can only take you through my journey as I consider and write a poem. Perhaps, this method will allow you to better understand my poems as well as all poetry.

Sometimes a poem is not as accessible to a poet, but is instead hiding somewhere deep inside an emotion. Often I will begin a poem simply because I saw something that makes me think of a line that carries an interesting sound. When I take this line and begin, I try to make the rest of the poem flow in a similar manner, dancing off of my tongue as the first line usually did for days. I often take a line to bed and dream about it, and wake to it in the morning, still unsure of what it will mean in completed poem.

> *tar feathers drape*
> *around your Tuscany face*

followed me for weeks. Sometimes I can only rid my mind of these phrases that incessantly repeat over and over, if I sit down with a pen and write a poem following the phrase. It is interesting that I have been known to cut the original phrase entirely out of a poem. Usually the phrase will haunt me until I pause and write, yet, occasionally a phrase will disappear on its own or continue to repeat even after I have written poetry. I am not sure if this is some divine sign informing me that I did not complete my task adequately, or if my tongue is only waiting for something else smooth to suck on.

But a poem seems like so much more to me than brilliant images and flowing verse. I have a poet friend whose images are concise and vivid, yet when I read her poetry I am not enthralled. On the contrary, I feel as though it was tightly constructed, so tightly developed and built that the walls that encase the poem block out any emotion and desecrate it. A poem with stark images alone cannot carry a reader to the end of it, if the poem is void of any experiencable emotion.

After investigating and dissecting, I still cannot simply explain how a poem connects unimaginable ideas and images and links them in a very real way. Perhaps, it is because I am out of practice in expository writing and was never that precise or eloquent, but often just want the theories to spill, and connect and flow as when one is writing poetry. The ability of a poem to connect ideas, yet move forward into another dimension has always bewildered me. When one is constructing an essay, one spits out a theory, and begins supporting it in order to divulge a linked theory that inevitably unwraps another theory, and eventually paints a proposal. However, a poem's construction is not so logical and outlined.

As I write poetry, ideas are joined and often I do not even question their juxtaposition until a reader does. After I have written a poem, it seems excessively expository. I may feel it is too obvious, yet a reader may still be lost in a poem that I thought was overly revealing. For example, a poem in which I planned to start at one point at the beginning of the poem and end at another provides a prime example. In *The Lavender Window*, a photograph is mysteriously connected to an old room I used to live in, which is connected to my father's visit, which is connected to my pregnancy and impending labor. However, the photograph was simply of a window and a chair. To myself, the connections made in this poem are not gigantic leaps, yet perhaps to a reader they may be unjustified connections. As a poet, taking this chance may be wonderful or could be detrimental. Poets face this risk in light of every poem they create as an expression.

In review of my thoughts, I don't think the connections I've made while briefly explaining my writing process adequately express the ideas I have been considering. I do not feel as though I have elicited any genuine emotions for you as the reader. Perhaps, I have at least allowed for some self-speculation in trade of a valid description and explanation of poetry. At the end of these slow and scattered pages, I hope I have at least brought you forward past the forward and onto my creative expression. Ahead *lies* my poetry, wrapped into tight balls, self-contained. In these poems you will find the definitive beginning and the unavoidable ending. In these poems, I die and in these poems, I am born.

Much Love,
LisaAnn

Contents

In The Swollen
Poetry

LisaAnn LoBasso

a touch of dew lies on the tips
the blue grass swaying as the waves
of a sea—back and forth

back and forth, the wind carrying you
gently
as a newborn

Jasmin LoBasso- Spencer

Two Week Pox Stupor

and they pop out, bubbling volcanic freaks.
This is Mary. On her head, that is Joe.
He's fat and round and his body protrudes
hard like a pregnant woman due last week.
Mary is minuscule, itchy, a pro
nag, hiding on her lid naked and lewd.

this is their peaches and cream corruption.
Joe's pals eat lard, fuck drunk socialite no's,
spawn midget puss babes and name one moondude.
The ladies dine and dance on cheap beer skin
and wake up scabbed nude.

Cocoons

1. Cherry
Tomatoes make your breasts grow
her uncle told us, but I ate them anyway.
He used to lie
on the sofa, cocoon me and squeeze my arm tight
as if he was testing for ripeness
testing my breasts in his breath.
I am not a tomato,
I don't even like tomatoes Uncle Jack.

2. Chamber
I search the strings to find Emily.
I know she is Emily
wrapped around her cello cocoon-like
but not touching the arched glistening wood body
her mime arms stiff, elbows raised.
She nods her head allegro andante allegretto.
Yes, I'm sure she is Emily, oceanbody waving.

3. My Daughter
Her lungs push up against her body.
He cocoons her lungs tight and the muscles freeze.
I've always imagined him male
that asthman god

6

lowering the guillotine over my baby's satin chest.
Will she be Elsie injecting adrenaline?
Will she be Elsie chasing Ignasio with silk knives?
Will she lie awake at night
clenching her jaw until her teeth madden?
I've always wanted her to be Emily
virtuoso and Victorian.

4. Grandmother

A blueice Victorian house lies
next to my mother's coral stucco home.
I want to buy it, fill it with antiques, wood glistening,
be a moment from my mother's cocoon.
I run to her like those advertisements of people
romantic couples in slow motion
with their arms spread so they swallow their lover
in their grasp.
My mother always ran backwards from Elsie in her ads
ran backwards from the east coast to the west
backwards from Elsie's envelope
adrenaline fists and tight teeth.

5. Doctor

The white willow balloons, a capsule
over my three-year-old body, peeking through the leaves.
My mother's voice strips Michael and Matt's

whispers as I pull up my pants fast.
As if I put the nail up my canal
as if I must hide
from the snakes spying through the satinwood
the snakes shedding their skin,
their slithering thin ghost-cocoons
behind them.

The Lavender Window

When I look at Solinsky's Lavender Window on my wall,
the wood chair in the middle of the white-paneled room
somehow looks similar to the dirty metal chair
that I painted rusty-red
on that night.
It was the night I stayed up past two
and painted the naked wood in the garage
rose and green and purple,
the rainbow of my father's ladder dreams.
That night, painting with a friend who was a little fast,
we brushed and rolled over frozen spiders, wet webs,
and a thick dust-mask. I tried to teach him to stroke, but
he brushed like a boy. And I never slept after.

Under the lavender window, the chair has a sloped leather seat
that's imprinted with a hard
young ass like the ones that mold ass-angels in snow
by Shasta where I lived when I was young and hard.

A day later I moved in the florescent garage
and strew extension cords
over cement steps, so I could have light at night
when I wrote.
When Winter came and rooftop-rain crawled through the cracks,
I was afraid the cat would die
so I locked her inside or let her hide in the safe womb

9

under the soggy bushes.
Once my father drove the desert road to see my obsession,
my wonderland.
He ravaged the garage and tore apart my snakes and rewired.
He said I could have killed myself, been found lying
in a tight little ball in the muddy puddles
that flooded my $300 home. And I shook the garage-door opener
in the misty air, reminding him that at least
I had an electric door.
I was worried about the cat.

Dad's head was glued to the box on the ceiling for hours
and when he came down to breathe, he tried to scurry off,
but I thought of tiny hands in electrical sockets
and asked him to stay for dinner, to stay to talk.
I cooked spaghettini with thick red sauce and stared
at the clumped sauce that looked foreign
to me now, like clotted afterbirth,
and told him that I had always wanted a girl,
one that would wrestle with me at bedtime until her lids
flickered and drooped blue and her rigid legs
went limp with shivering laughter.

And when he finally spoke, he said he never understood my art
anyway.
And I knew this girl was grinding and weeping
in my womb. I could feel
the liquids pass between us
and I imagined the spread-leg ache contracting both

our bodies, and the sweat that would swell my tongue.
And I said this is for you Dad,
and his fork froze and I said
whoever you are, this is for you.

Astute as a Two-Year Old

and she is the quietest baby
sitting on the sofa.
her hands gripping the cushion,
she widens her eyes and shakes
a silent no,
so familiar to women,
while the daddy she loves twists
her mommy's shirt collar
and drops her down
like she is nothing more
than a sack of rotten potatoes.

and this is in the morning
when they said they wouldn't
fight.
after the black and blues of cops
and anger,
and ruined transmissions slipping
under white wine.
and this is the morning.
how they will make up
and raise her and teach her
to meet a man who will peel
an apple for her. who will
move out when their marriage
is too putrid
and bruised.

and she is the quietest baby
sitting on the sofa.
her hands ripping the cushion
with untrimmed fingernails.
she widens her tear ducts
and shakes a silent.
shake of her mother.
shake of her grandmother.
and her grandmother's mother.
her grandmother's grandmother.

shake of herself
when she is grown into a woman
breakable and limp,
like her doll who sits
next to her still, wide-eyed.
silent.

a silent no
so familiar to women.
and she is the quietest baby.

Graceland

They think they can find him.
So they pack up the tan station wagon and promise
to scratch psychedelic flowers on it in a day or two
if they haven't found him.

At the Chevron station, sparkling bikinis spill out
of the flowered station wagon and they smile rosy strawberry
and wonder if they should go to Goodwill for a hall tree
and they promise the attendant
love or their clothes in memory of Elvis.
They haven't found him yet.

They draw rosy-flowered curtains on the windows
and sleep in the back seat, front seat and floor board
ten minutes each—after the policeman shot
the flashlight in their eyes at three a.m.
and told them he wasn't on the beach and they'd have to find
someplace else to sleep,
after
the thorned-branch's backswing poked one
in the eye as they ran from howling coyotes,
and they decided to sleep so maybe he would send a dream
and point them to Memphis.

In the morning of the naked bulb in the Chevron bathroom
they wash each other's hair in the sink

and garnish their faces with gold glitter
and slip on silver swimsuit tops
after deciding that real clothes would weigh down their hajj.
Outside in the blue and red twinkling of the electric-neon
Chevron sign, they pack up their clothes and smile
their all-shook-up smiles
and gyrate their pink pelvises at the attendant.
Through his hound-dog tongue he asks where they spent the night.
Graceland, they say as they hand him their suitcases,
Elvis wants you to have these.
So they pack their bodies into the wagon and promise
to get to the Mecca before morning
so they'll have someplace to sleep.
They know they can find him.

Denial at Noon Within the Teal Playpen

The house is confused.
Spaghetti is snarled around peanut butter apples.
Panties are entangled in dry typewriter ribbons.
None are wet or speckless,
Or misty with blue Kool-Aid,
Or whimsical with french vanilla silk strips.
None are twirled
Around windows or balconies,
Or across entrances or spinning stair rails.
No undies are wrapped around wonderland chairs,
Swirling yellow and purple and neon pink.
None are painted in Christmas crimson,
Or satin-nude newborn birthdays.
The man is not eating
Sweet tangerines syruped in hot fudge,
Or tender steak on gold-lined plates.
He will not dream
Of green teddies or pitch periwigs
Draped around tight nipples.
But for a minute the baby,
Trapped beneath elongated toys with fuzzy teeth,
Licks One Man Dog and bites
The Gorilla's tongue
In meshed neglect.

Upon a Sick Child

She cries because she can't breathe
and now she breathes even less.
She will not eat bananas
tapioca pudding or chocolate
berry-covered cookies.
Only water and grape-stinging medicine.
And he says let her alone,
after my tenth trip to the nursery
to console her pink swollen eyes
and red runny nose.

let her alone.

This is the time she should learn
to go to sleep without her security cup.
Without water.

let her alone.

They have to meet the man at noon,
and my father says Bear—
their Australian Shepherd pup—
has to learn sometime. He's chained in
105 degrees and knocks the water bowl over
for the tenth time.
And my parents leave

him without water for an hour,
because he has to learn sometime.
And they return to a beautiful
black and white carcass.
But what was left to do?
They could not keep him in the house—
he would rotten the air in hours.
And he was too voluptuous
and thick-furred to lie in the weather.
There was nothing left
but to bury him.

let her alone.
She cries because she can't breathe
and now she breathes less.

So last week my father, he ties the Shepherd pup,
Baby Baby, in the blue and white pick-up
and backs it against the fence.
She's in heat.
He doesn't want her to mate
and I am to call the vet
to ask the length of inconvenience.
Three weeks she will want and want
and push.
But on the first night he says
let her alone.

let her alone.

And she wants and wants
and thirsts and cries because she cannot
breathe.
And I am glad in the morning,
glad that I am not a man
finding her neck stretched in the chain,
her mouth wide frozen in her cry.
And there is nothing left
but to bury her.

She cries because she cannot breathe.
let her alone.
And now she breathes even less.
let her alone.
And in the morning who
will lift her from the wooden crib
and wipe her crusted nose
and lay a hand across her still chest?
who will bury her?
who will bury us?
because there will be nothing left
except to stuff her small body
tight into the crevice of my breasts,
and press us into the ground
hidden from the weather.

D—

　　　　It is midday of a day sometime next month. We
　　　　　　are alive. I am
writing since it is almost a year since we began
　　　　　speaking. I am
writing after my twelfth (drink) promise to write
with a package of pictures, but I am (not drunk)
　　　　　not enclosing the photos, not this time.
I am
writing in place of a poem I must search
　　　　for somewhere, but the house
is too hot and has eaten it. I believe
　　　　my home is bothered, but the doctor will no
longer make house calls in this time.

　　　　My
pistachio baby is crawling in circles
　　　　with her eyes pulled back in her head.
Her face is shining and her mouth is drawn wide
　　　　like Jack Lunatic Nicholson, only
she has eight teeth and porcelain skin.
I wait
for your call under flowered covers
at night after you have probably already gone
　　　　to bed, because of the time difference.
I wonder

where your hands are while your husband sleeps
      next to you, like mine.
My baby has promised me she will walk
this month, and I am keeping my palms pressed.
I do not wish her to walk
      for any reason other than the echoing phone
full of relatives' ringing tired lines.

I am
writing in place of the last six (sick) mornings I have
      woken thinking it too early to phone.
Later in the day, I realize it is three hours
later
but then you are somewhere stretched
      on a Long Island highway, I imagine,
at a number I had written down—
      but the house has eaten it too in its hunger.
I will write again, sending the photos next time.
My baby practices hugs. I believe
she sends you one. I am
considering the time difference and the distance,
and considering the holiday shuffle
and the number of little blue mailboxes
      between here and N.Y.

I hope you are alive,
and wish you red

holidays. I pray for the quick arrival
of my letter and a visit sometime
          within the next twelve years. I am

                                        All love,
                                        Your Cousin

Fantoccini Step-Father

You take her hand first
when you walk through the chipped
green door and tip-toe dance past me
on white linoleum,
with smoke oozing out my pores.
Cold meat stains my palms
and drenches
my dress in its raw juices.

You two talk about something I
can smell sweet through the carrots,
and pretend you don't see my
twisted eyes arcing through doorways.
I fawn to hear the falsetto patter
of your mimicry tracing
across her full cheeks.

She opens wide to wet kiss your nose
and scratches your face,
as her arm moves clicking like a drunk
marionette maneuvering
toward your eyes. She clenches your words,
tugging on your goatee.
I watch the two of you
in the dusk, you waddling behind her,
your head anchored over her thirty inches.

She walks in a stupor, her hands in yours,
like you're her animator.
I click the carrots, click the celery
on the cutting board,
and string stick-figure kabobs.

The two of you whisper staggering secrets,
and smile white quiet
when you look at me cooking in the kitchen.
And I can only muse
behind my wooden simper.
I wonder if your words sound something
sugary, something salivating,
like the lines my father told me.
The lines I never remember,
except at two in the morning when I smile
in my sleep with my arms stretched
above my head, moving awkwardly with my
phantom Punchinello.

tar feathers drape

around your Tuscany face
and I can feel the hot licking,
my inner ear bubbling.
I swoosh
to the inner rhythm, stop
and show you the beaded
gown I bought ten years ago
before I knew you or my dripping
daughter. I was just thirteen.
but the long elaborate panel
made me feel svelte
and ready.
and the woman said I
looked like a Russian princess
with a train of admirers all
needy and taut and young.
I have kept it hidden
in tissue under my bed
and now when I move the folds
black and green growth peeks out
from its ivory skin whispering
secret smells of years and years
that I want to strip
so that it will whiten
and whip when I spin.
and your tar feathers will
flip and ask.
and I will

be ready.
ready
in veiled mesh of mold
and microscopic holes.

Cribbage

This tampon worms out, trying to escape
the oppression of my taut kiss,
as I wiggle away from sweaty limpid arms
smashing my sore breasts.

I have walked to the toilet
more than four times tonight with
nothing coming, only gurgling
in my lungs and intestines—the sharp
cramps of menstruation.

I spend hours in the blue air of the t.v.,
the mamamamadada mumbling
silent in the antique yellow crib.
Her belly bubbling rhythmically
under the pink and white striped womb,
that keeps her warm, protected from thick air
trying to creep under cotton covers.

My belly swollen with water and needles.
I do not pass blood or feces,
only sputtering that rumbles in the dark.
I am sure I will wake you and the baby
with my candlelight coughs.
Mucus will come and you will try to kiss
me when I am spitting tissue and prying

for my flesh under sharp nails and stiff
midnight-chapped lips.

In a few more hours, the house will rise
and I will want to close my eyes
under the heat and the sticky baby.
But she will call mamamama to me
for a five-a.m.-fresh diaper,
and you will pinch my nipple
and I will have to carry you both.

Even after I have spent half the thick night
planning my inch-tip-toe-inch escape,
before my body gives birth to something
wild and flailing.
something strident and glowing.
something pink and tight
as my dry wadded tampon
half-eaten, half-free
in the orange grip of dawn.

Melt

sweetsweetsweet
sweet
wa　　　　ter
me　　　　lon
sweet dancing red
　　　　　　　　along your tongue
tickling
sweetsweetsweet
sweet
wa　　　　ter
me　　　　lon
swirling through teeth
　　　　　　　　　blood with black
screaming
sweetsweetsweet
ru　　　　by
　　　　　raindrops with night

sweee　　　eeet
wa　　　　ter
me　　　　lon
longing me
　　　　　into your mouth
stroking
sweetsweetsweet
calling me home

sweet man   ip
                              ulating undulation
to sweetsweetsweet
sweet
wa   ter
me   lon

Dry Season

Yesterday I called at two
reaching
out dry like a cactus.

Yesterday you still
scraped through my head
when the receiver said you
were missing.
I knew you were there and I
missing don't want
to sleep anymore.

I am like a camel
humped and parched
and dry.
I can feel the heat prickling
out of my lashes
and I wish I could sleep on this
arid silence.
I still hear you long-stemmed and sly
vibrating off my dead white walls
and out of
Morrison's glass penis.

Yes, I can still milk my memories
and make black pudding

to offer you
when I call you.

But it's not you
I've just forgotten
since you've laced the lines
with doubt
covered my mouth
and splintered my hips.

I had forgotten that I pushed you off
let you crawl and dehydrate lies
to get away.

But I guess cacti never die
even when I'm calling someone else
at two, two years later.

And my heart still collapses
like a melting marshmallow angel
drinking languid liquid
of you.

Elsie In Us

Let's say she had glistening golden tresses
that twinkled when she hung
her head out of the window screaming
across the street at my mother
in the summer.

Suppose she had blue blue eyes deep
and deep and cold like
the blizzard nights of Knickerbocker
Avenue in winter.

Did she laugh the laugh that runs
through my family like a hysterical child,
with a twinge of evil
as my mother fell?

Did she heave and falter, the adrenaline
needle bubbling, like a junkie jeweled
when she desperated to find her fix
alone, after her husband's heart
just stopped one day because maybe it was old
and tired and crazed
and it sped up swift right before?

I imagine Elsie walking fast and nervous
from the window to the kitchen table
twitching her lonely fingers.

33

I watch her hold my mother by the neck
clasped like a plastic doll, cut
my mother's hair short and perm it
tight and hard and delicately
primp the collar of the flowered doll dresses
she'd bought on Myrtle Avenue.

I hear her in my hand-slapping bantering
daughter and search for her in my father
as he grabs his hair at the roots and digs.
I look for her in the silence of my mother's
glance and triangle cheeks
and the bulging of her whites,
like iced insane powder addicts,
when she slaps ignorant
department store clerks with her eyes.

I dream of her at night. Dreams
I don't remember but imagine
that they must be something like sweat,
me strapped across her apartment,
stretched on her grave.
I find her hidden among brows
in passing faces on the street
that I follow for miles.
I pillage for her every hour,
lie with her, forever severed,
hold her cold body blue

when my daughter's arms grasp my neck,
see her *Ich Ich* face, smell her under my
pink skin. Elsie, Elsie, my
shrinking violet, your open face,
your stark smell.

You Come

                    back to me at DMV
your tight triangle cheeks   my lover
entranced in a liquid fire   and motivation
made of white dust   my lover
who pissed in corners of brown shag rug
I watch your jaw click   the muffled slap
of your saliva seeping inside   in my
new lover   as he rattles and rambles
in his hypnotic sleep   the same sleep
that stole you
I wonder if you two are the same skinny man
if I am twenty again   asking for piss
to wash me   with your yellow love
I wonder   am I there again
crouched in the corner   crawling
and licking   for you   for something
under   the staunchy shag
where you hid my grace   with your absurd
foul love

For Micca and Her
Photograph in Her House

You do not have red hair.
But if you were my red-headed man
would I have slept with you in the house
where her picture throbs? The heart
pumping—pushing and sucking the glass
in and out rhythmically.
And I am not married
to you or anyone.

You do not have red hair.
But if you were my red-headed man would I
have slept with you?
Would I have seen your figure rise
magically to disappear into foggy
dream air. Air that is not
yours or mine. In
a room that does not belong to us.
And I am not married to you
or anyone.

You do not have red hair. My red-headed man
is fiery. A luxury.
He would come and go in a slick stream
like Evel Knievel. He would come
once and go

once like a storm. A hurricane.
And he would wear a mask
like the Lone Ranger, sweeping me
to safety and vanishing before I
could thank him.
But our union is as absurd
as Lois Lane's love for Superman
—never consummated.

If you were my red-headed man
you would be
my hero, my mystery.
You would be solid like the rocks
you climb
and soft like the cherub daughters
you created.
And if you were him
we would meet one sweet sweet
night and never come together again.

But I am not married to you or anyone.
And you are not my mystical man,
my horrid lover
in a house of delicate vases.
Those vases hold flowers for your wife
and would crack
at the sight of my naked body. No, I am not the nymph
nimbling through halls of her house—
transformed to a fertile forest.

You are not my red-headed man. I do
not lick you like strawberry. You do
not spoon me like savory
ice cream.
The gods do not mesh our bodies
together, like grapevines entwined,
but play cruel games,
flinging you at me once a year
like a boomerang.
And each time I eat you.
All of you
like a bulimic eats everything.
And once I have
expelled you,
you withdraw
leaving me vacuous, an anorexic until
you return.

And I am not
married to you.
And you do not
have red hair.
It is vanilla
blonde, long.
And I have
swallowed it
and choked
too often.

18th Street

a cappa luna
mountain hurls over the glass
my shunted stomach

legs crossed over two
times, skinny spider caffeine
tunneled bitter thin

forty minutes limp
full yellow walls moldable
mochamon slim straws

Sugarloaf

In Sugarloaf, in the center of 102
acres, her twenty-three inch body
watched trees grow, saw streams
flow below the earth, heard wet
sugar dripping from branches where
whispering birds shot from waterfall
　　　　to pine.

A poem always has rape in it.
Incest.
Molestation crawling from the walls.
Anger scrawled in a dark place, in a poem.

When she turned, I didn't answer her gurgle.
Her white skin, pasting her body together,
　　　　tightened as she smiled.
And I smiled. What is this?
Everyone needs peace.

Yes, from the fear in a hollow place, in a poem.
Her syrupy body glimmers in the daylight.
Her eyes glaze over as the fog creeps around
　　　　her cheeks whining red.
She licks my nose, nodding her football head
　　　　when I laugh.
Her small hands clasp my hair, ripping it.

I stare at her lightbulb body.
How could anyone not love her body?
How could any man love her body?
She is my baby, my daughter dripping
sweet from her mouth like sap from leaves.
Her eyes are blue-grey like the pewter sky.

I don't doubt for a minute that she loves her life.
Her grandfather blasts Gatorade cans off fallen
        logs where I spot deer tracks.
Her grandmother wipes her diamond chin
as white slop flows like a river.
Why can't life be like the forest, she crinkles
her question, her forehead growing old
        like her mother.
I flatten my face in the icy creek
that dries up in seconds. The trees fall.
Birds boomerang into oak trunks and crash
        to the sad earth.

I am still mesmerized by her body,
its picturesque innocence dripping
sweet square sugarloaf, I almost cannot
hear the roar of the monster
        eating the mountain
filled with rape, incest
molestation in the dark silent squirrel holes.

Ersatz Mother

I don't remember the water remembering.
There's a creek on the land, springing from
a corner chunk,
a tiny twenty acre square you'd smooth
       to erase the protrusion.

It comes up right there, on that
       wart.
It bubbles cold, milky-marsh, and then travels
       light across the forest.

Because it comes up from the center, up from
below the dirt, is that how the water knows?
I don't remember it knowing how to feed
my Sugarloaf oatmeal wet, without letting
her swallow the plastic spoon
       she gnaws on.
I don't remember: does the water gag and engulf
aspirin as it wipes her human-like?
Does it feather her face and butterfly her bottom?
Does it somehow wash her over with all the red
       knowledge of the apple?

Will it wash her pouring forth histories of nice
       uncles at eleven?
Will it cleanse her releasing secrets

of towering men tying her at nineteen?
Will it embody her, deem her untouchable,
by man or the gods, hissing over the rocks
that she is beautiful and pure and clean?
Will it hurl itself up, waking an utterly
              beast-like instinct
shielding her with the magic of the white dome?

Then
It is her mother.
It must take her now
before my face cracks firenight in the wind.
It must take her now and tell her
              the words it never told me.
I was raised by a woman who knows
              nothing
of black shimmering nights trickling
and traveling light. We carry round redwood logs.
Fat back-breaking logs that mock labor's hollow tunnel-ache.

And I cannot be the christening creek
whispering watery webs to Jasmin. And my murmur
              is whitewashed with screams
so that she may not come close
              to the fine white lines.
And I cannot wash her insides or bleed her blue.
And I know what the willows confess.
And I cannot forgive them.

You're Always
Talking of Killing

i'm going to take a gun and shoot his balls
why is he always so close to me?

can i shoot her, hun?
she doesn't know what an albatross is

why is she crying again?
i'm going to shoot someone

it's hot and i can't sleep caffeine
do you want me to kill him

for that thing three years ago?
there was penetration and i love you

i could send gas through the mail
and it would only be one more

dead. who would know?
only you and the albatross i suppose.

Sweeping

My husband, he tells me what to do
and I offer my non-answer nod down.
I watch dust crumbs sweep the room
and straw brush oriental rug.
My husband, that's what I call him
even though we don't wear gold
and I never walked white or shoved
cake in his face, he still tells me
what is proper and I still
fold his shirts and ask
for some allowance on Mondays,
even though We pretend it is different.
My mother doesn't admit that my father
never cooked for her until last week.
She is 44 and in bed, too weak
to move, and he makes ham and eggs
and discovers teflon.

My husband, he will cook for me
when I'm 60 and in the hospital
suffering from dementia or consumption.
He will make pizza, his head burning
in the oven, cheese skating
across the blue kitchen floor
and sausage in his nostrils. His imaginary
crumbs will chase ants

on ceramic tile, and he will complain
about the invisible bits
in between his toes. I'll apologize
for not sweeping with my long-arm
broom, that reaches from the third-floor
ward to our house in the Southwest.
I'll rave about the pizza
when he pulls a piece from the box
for himself,
us sitting in the ice-white room,
smelling sterile sheets
and sausage I hate.
He'll bring me leftover pizza
the next day and monotone
his 'love yous' across the room,
cold pizza in his teeth, in between
the yellow story of his kitchen slavery,
he forgets he has told me. And I'll smile
the patients' smile.

My husband, if I decide to leave him
and We go dancing, I'll meet some handsome
man with slim legs and gathering arms.
He will wrap around my waist and pull
me close to move against the music.
He will tell me I have a nice figure
for having a baby already, and say
he couldn't tell when we met.
We will go to auraistic Olive Garden dinners

and he will whisper that I'm beautiful,
the way my hair sweeps my eyes.
And in three months, I'll be folding
his shirts and ironing flying saliva.

who else is going to
who else will rear the baby
who else will wash the dishes
fold and clean and cook
who else will run the house smooth

We will never admit that when
We get home from work, he isn't
there shining the tile, wiping
the baby's butt and frying bacon
because who needs to know

who needs to know how my house moves
through the day
who needs to know how I survive

My husband, he tells me
and I offer
my non-answer nod and my patient smile.
And I continue to sweep.

Lovers

Twenty-five hats line the white wall
of twenty-five women.
When I wear silk and walk on institution steps
I am someone other than
when I am home in pink bunny pajamas.

now am I the woman who loves cooking
domestic harmony?
am I the woman who is wisped into evil sex?
now am I the poet in green velvet, peasant
rims hiding my eyes?
am I the princess in an elaborate headdress?
or am I the machismo man in a green kepi?

And how many women can I be
and how many lovers can I have?
Every time I move I change my name.
And every time I speak of an exquisite
man or woman,
he is the love of my life,
she is the love of my life.
who I was meant to be
with.
with him.
with her.
and no one else.

A.M. Appointment
at the Clinic

It's itchy up there
and the doctor says I have something,
PID. And I spread my legs on asexual stirrups
and wait for him to enter
the room,
and tell me my cunt is sacred enough
to fuck my man.
He asks if it hurts when
he wiggles his finger.
I want to say, I don't know doc,
did you sprain your finger,
but I just nod my head and squirm,
squinching my eyes and tensing
my thighs as he pokes.

He says certainly I'm itchy.
Can you feel it doc, with your index finger?
Oh, yes maybe you've felt this odium before,
you were a woman last time, weren't you, doc?
And he says yes yes
the antibiotics have contributed to my yeast
infection, and holds up discharge
like he's in session. Here's Exhibit A,
your honor.

I modestly pull my legs back and mash
them together, and wipe lubrication
from my thighs. I slip
on my skirt.

In the waiting room, there's my man
reading Seventeen,
not watching our baby climb across the window
sill. What's wrong with you?
Nothing, nothing, I say waiting
room eyes, like a jury
perched stiff
on machismo stirrups, ready to stick
the speculum inside.

I have PID. The doctor
says you need to take medication too.
Oh does he? My man spits.

He asks if I got the Depo shot and I
say no, I'm thinking about it. It
makes you nauseous and there's possible
weight gain.
What's there to think, well then
Norplant then.
And I say no, I don't want anything in my body, and he
says what the Hell, stick it in,
it lasts five years and I
say no, I don't want an IUD,

there's chance of urinary tract
infection and sterility.
And he says Hell, stick it
in, I don't want any more kids.
And I say, it's my body.
He says no, it's my body.
And I tug at my wrist,
it's my body.

But my man insists we need something,
don't want any more spoiled brats
clinging to the thigh.
And I ask the forbidden question,
staring at his silent rubber lips.
Oh, wait
they're uncomfortable
and oh yeah, it takes you
too long to come.
Yes, yes makes you want to sleep,
if you can't do it in two short strokes,
just stick it in and wiggle
for a second.
Yes, yes I understand the side
effects are too great,
I'd forgotten.

And what the Hell is PID anyway, Hun,
who'd you get that from? Who you
been spreading your legs for lately?

Retreat

When I was missing for three days
few wondered what happened to me.
It isn't unusual for a poet
to disappear like stars in the city sky.

and would I come back Monday
to talk alliteration emotion
would I come back
to reveal spit and sarcasm
would I appear in thick air
to pin my hair back secure
like the history in my poetry

When I was missing for three days
I thought of writing,
my pen across the blue horizon line.
It isn't unusual for a poet
to disappear like stars in the city sky.

and would I walk straight Monday
to swap fancy visions
would I walk back
to sit silent in the rocked meaning
would I appear in thick air
to pin my hair back secure
and nod my head down to begin

When I was missing for three days,
I thought of beginning lines.
I thought of writing exercises
and repeating lines.
I thought of blocks and how
my hair so tight back
hurt my head when I was writing.
But there was no other way,
it would get in the way.

When I was missing for three days
few wondered what happened to me.
And upon my return, I told them
of miscarriages and death
I told them of nervous
breakdowns and squeezing brains.
I told them of shock
treatment and rebirth
in my poetry,
that appeared thick like sweet
mist in the night air.
But my husband knew I was always
in a wood cabin at Big Bear,
not writing, but sleeping
       It isn't unusual for a poet
with some man in the mountains.
       to disappear like stars in the city sky.
Few wondered what happened to me.

On the Shelf

You know I have work to do myself
and sometimes coffee will not do at six a.m.
But now you'll have to learn to sew for yourself.

Take down the white needle from the shelf
and begin with the floral skirt, it needs a hem.
You know I have work to do myself.

The Singer's clean and sleek, but dust the filth
off the Brother if you'd rather a him.
But now you'll have to learn to sew for yourself.

There's light by that window, and a glib elf
comes at one o'clock if the slacks are not sewn.
You know I have work to do myself.

My nails decay on emery, my health
delicate petals on that skirt trim,
and now you'll have to learn to sew for yourself.

I am not well, and we do not have wealth
so get up, and take this button.
You know I have work to do myself.
But now you'll have to learn to sew for yourself.

Dim

I take the pan down and it
is dusty and the stove's fire stale. What

was I planning? There's no one
to cook for, you're dead, Jasmin

married with teenagers of her own.
They promise her they'll come home

early, the same way she promised
me fifteen years ago and never did.

I nurse the teflon and take eggs
from the fridge and scramble, legs

weak and tired from standing too long.
I add chorizo and fry bacon wrong,

nice and soft, not your crisp exact rulers.
I take orange juice and pour as

if you would choose juice over milk,
and I meticulously fork

the food onto my tongue,
desperate for my groove, custom

In The Swollen   *LisaAnn LoBasso*

for me to play the paltry housewife
while you sit by the window, life

passing you by from nine to midday,
while you clock a vampire's day.

They Should Let It Go By

Don't let them go. The yellow
socks bought five months in anticipation
before you knew what it was.
And how you remember rocking
the cat named after your Aunt
Dewellen the first few weeks, night
after night yowling for her mother
somewhere dark around the corner
in those crack-crying apartments
off Sycamore Street. Although,
it never really was Sycamore,
but that always sounded prettier—
the way you liked to remember.

Don't let them go. The yellow
socks bought five months in anticipation
before you knew what it was.
And how you remember a sweet red
undulation of passion as you forced
down his arms and felt sore breasts weeks
later and knew he must have
come. You must have come
but you don't remember, you just like
to tell the story of an earth-
shaking, reverent conception.

That's what you like to tell her.
It sounds much prettier—
the way you like things.

Don't let them go. The yellow
socks bought five months in arrest
before you knew who she was.
And how you remember sleeping
on your feet those nights you waited
for your own mother to shrivel white
into nothing. And panic dripped
from your armpit, from your pitted
stomach, that Mother lunaticed
like them all. And one
day she would try to tie
herself to the top shelf too—
neat and pretty, the way she

liked. And you would take her feet
and tuck them in yellow socks
too small. And she would
don't
and she would
let them
and she would
go

Last Night

You freeze with your angry fuck-me sex,
having no idea about conception,
having no idea what's solid
and what's soft in my ice blue holes.

Everything that's hard is crumbling
under your weight
squished flat under you
like a lonely cockroach in eighths.

It's orgasmic the way your lower lip
drools and drops
the way you're oblivious to the mechanical movements
and sucked into the drools and drawls

Of your flittering, ejaculating lids
red and raw
and closed to the suffocating cockroach,
warm and wet with its juices
warm and wet and gone
under you.

Devil's Golf Course And
Dylan Thomas' Stalker

The muted alluvial fans
inspire the salt creek pupfish
to swim in dense waters
where minerals converge

                And honored among alluvial fans
                I am the prince of salt beds
                And the force that dries
                my mouthing stream dries
                my red blood
                And I am the pupfish

He rises from dormancy
and glows bright acid
of Artist's Palate—richer
than Gold Canyon refracting
Tut's tomb

                And then like a wanderer white
                I was all shining
                The sea gathered again
                So it must have been the birth
                And honored in the sun born over
                and over in my heedless ways

He gulps the toxic water
of the crystallite white sea
And the salt spreads
its filigreed fan

         And I must enter again the round
         Zion of the water bead
         And the synagogue of saline waters
         Shall I let pray
         and sow my salt seed
         In the least valley of sackcloth.

My Name Is Nira

it is the name
given to a soft-wrinkled, pink-skinned girl
an hour old, a name for
a tight twenty-year one
with strawberry blonde curls and faint freckles.
And I still try to hear her breathing.

it is a name
an excited eighteen-year-old
picks for her first, for motherhood,
a name she wanted when all her life
she's been called Judith, like the Sister
in the Motherhouse she longed to join
when she was fourteen and frightened
as her chest exploded overnight.
And I still try to hear her breathing.

I know the story of bursting breasts
and burning skirts
and a vagina so fixed
that thrusting seems forced
and foreign
like a slow, silent film, the body
still cramping
and contracting nine months after the act.
the body still laid out.
the head turned tense with teeth marks on the lips.
the body still with spread legs,

still aching and tearing the first time.
the body still.
And I still try to hear her breathing.

I know the story: wondering
what she will bestow upon
her pig-skinned wonder
to take her to a better destiny.
and I name her Judith
in hopes of pasty skin patience
and mousy hovering hair.
And I still try to hear her breathing.

I know the story of waiting
all night when she's fifteen, and out,
probably pinned to a wall
or a car seat in dark country.
and hoping it's not burning country.
it's not burning,
that she only broke down on a bright, busy
street on the way home from Baker Branch.
And I still try to hear her breathing.

My name is Nira, but call me
Judith. I know
strawberry beauty and petulant impatience.
I know angry lust and legs.
I know the story of repeated history.

I know her sweet wrinkled skin
in my nostrils,

my daughter,
while my skin wrinkles dry and hard and old
my daughter not
coming, not coming back after fifteen.
and I still try to inhale her skin, taste her
in my nostrils,
my daughter no.
in her caged crib,
And I still try to hear her breathing.

At Night

she lies awake listening for
a ringing phone waiting
for a siren from the muted television.
>The baby's breathing is rapid, fired.
>She talks loud in a language of goo.

She thinks of wiping and sweeping,
but longs to sleep like a man—wanting
her breathing moving her chest
up and down rhythmically as if she
is not breathing at all.
>It is time to pull on electric cords,
>and knock antique vases onto the floor.

It amazes her how much a sleeping man
looks dead. That is
if he is not snoring.
>She walks over crashing porcelain
>and glass and cuts
>her feet, and cries.

But like all nights, she lies awake patting
the blanket down around her prepared
body, tucking and tucking and waiting.
>The blood is thick and comes fast
>like the pitapat
>hot on her tongue.
>It is time to somersault on sofas
>and rattle crib bars.

And if there is a noise.

    It is time to siren-scream and hyena-laugh

    and wriggle legs.

If a car wisps down the street or a shadow

knocks on the door,

she jumps to check the circumstances.

And leaves it to the floating phantoms.

    And she stomps

    and tumbles on her ass. It is time to contort

    her tongue to a new stumbling squall.

And retucks and waits.

    She bites her mother's nipple

    and laughs. It is time

    to tenderly butt heads like kissing coneheads.

But it is like all nights.

A noise never comes,

and she lies corpse-straight in bed

mesmerized by the silence.

    And she slams her head into cement.

About The Author

LisaAnn LoBasso, born in California in 1970, created songs to occupy her mind while traveling throughout the U.S. as a child. She didn't know then that the poet in her burned to stay on the road performing. Intent to remember the once revered role of poetry and the universal connections through verse, she takes fine art poetry into higher performance expectations, sometimes incorporating elements of music and performance art, and often integrating literary arts elements into mixed-media art installations.

Often just on the peripheral of the performance circle while straddling the poetry cliques of academia, LisaAnn attempts to walk the fine line of powerful literary art that is at the same time accessible, while keeping her eyes off the page and interacting with her audience. Refusing to categorize her poetry style as either academic or performance, you will find her most at home among artists.

LisaAnn considers poetry an art without age, the most powerful poetry originating from simple words, simple ideas and simple verse; when simplicity mixes with emotion, the most moving, passionate and mighty poetry is born.

Her work is often associated with women's issues and erotica and she is known for her powerful and dramatic readings. After 18 years experience, she is still referred to as *the girl* and has been called a "poetry minstrel" by *Las Vegas City Life Weekly*; her readings branded sexy and provocative on the East and West coasts.

LisaAnn studied photography and literature at the University of California, Berkeley and earned her Creative Writing degree from the University of California Riverside. Currently, she resides in Bakersfield, California with her husband and two daughters.

She is an *Artist in Residence* teaching poetry throughout Kern County. *In The Swollen* is her first book of poetry.

Printed in the United States of America
10 9 8 7 6 5 4 3 2 1